OUR DAILY BREAD FOR KIDS™

BIBLE
QUIZZES
& GAMES

People in God's Amazing Story

CRYSTAL BOWMAN & TERI McKINLEY

Our Daily Bread
Publishing™

Our Daily Bread for Kids: Bible Quizzes & Games—People in God's Amazing Story

© 2018 by Discovery House (Our Daily Bread Publishing)

Illustrations by Luke Flowers and © 2016 by Discovery House

Interior design by Michael J. Williams

ISBN: 978-1-916718-40-1

Printed in Europe

21 22 23 24 25 26 27 / 9 8 7 6 5 4 3

OUR DAILY BREAD FOR KIDS
BIBLE QUIZZES & GAMES

Hey, there! How exciting that you have this book! You're going to learn some important things about several people in the Bible, and you'll have fun while you learn.

These pages are filled with quizzes and puzzles that focus on characters from the beginning of the Bible to the end. Some of the puzzles may challenge your brain power, so use the Bible verse hints if you need help. Each quiz is followed by a related picture puzzle, a word search, and a crossword. All of the answers are found in the back of the book.

Are you ready? Let's go! Have fun as you learn more about the people in God's amazing story.

THE FIRST FAMILY

The Bible begins with the book of Genesis, which tells how God created a very good and beautiful world. In Genesis, we also learn about Adam and Eve, the first people who lived on earth. They had many children, grandchildren, and great-grandchildren.

WHAT DO YOU KNOW
ABOUT THE VERY FIRST PEOPLE?

Look up the Bible references if you need help with an answer!

1. **What did Adam and Eve do that messed up the world God made? (Genesis 3:6)**
   a) they didn't take care of the animals
   b) they forgot to water the garden
   c) they picked the flowers
   d) they ate some fruit that God told them not to eat

2. **What kind of work did Cain, the first child born on earth, do? (Genesis 4:2)**
   a) he was a farmer
   b) he was a shepherd
   c) he made tents
   d) he fixed computers

3. **What kind of work did Cain's younger brother, Abel, do? (Genesis 4:2)**
   a) he made pottery
   b) he was a shepherd
   c) he was a hunter
   d) he was a writer

4. **What happened that made Cain angry? (Genesis 4:4-5)**
   a) his plants wilted in the sun
   b) birds ate his fruit
   c) God was not pleased with his offering
   d) his brother took some of his vegetables

5. **What did Cain do because of his anger? (Genesis 4:8)**
   a) he ran away from home
   b) he stole Abel's sheep
   c) he killed his brother, Abel
   d) he burned his garden

6. **What was the name of Adam and Eve's third son, born after Abel? (Genesis 5:3)**
   a) Joshua
   b) Benjamin
   c) Samuel
   d) Seth

7. **What happened to Enoch, a descendant of Adam who loved God? (Genesis 5:24)**
   a) he became a ruler
   b) he became sick and died
   c) God took him up to heaven
   d) he became rich and famous

8. **Enoch's son Methuselah lived longer than any other person. How many birthdays did he have? (Genesis 5:27)**
   a) 580
   b) 650
   c) 789
   d) 969

Find the answers on page 141

Make as many words as you can out of the letters in

METHUSELAH

_____   _____

_____   _____

_____   _____

_____   _____

_____   _____

_____   _____

_____   _____

_____   _____

_____   _____

CROSSWORD PUZZLE

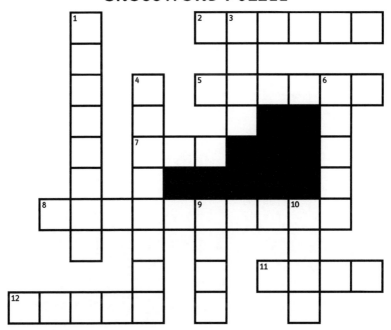

ACROSS

2. Someone who grows fruits and vegetables
5. God's home
7. The name of the first woman (Genesis 3:20)
8. The oldest man who ever lived (Genesis 5:27)
11. The first child ever born (Genesis 4:1)
12. God created the whole _____ for us to enjoy

DOWN

1. The first family had many _____
3. The second son born into the first family (Genesis 4:2)
4. A person who takes care of sheep
6. He walked and talked with God (Genesis 5:22)
9. The son born after Abel died (Genesis 5:3)
10. The name of the first man (Genesis 3:20)

Find the answers on page 141

WORD SEARCH
Can you find all the words?
Words may be forward, backward, or up-and-down.

ENOCH	ABEL	DESCENDANTS
FAMILY	ADAM	FIRST
METHUSELAH	EVE	FRUIT
CAIN	SETH	VEGETABLES

```
A V L O B A I F L E H U
D E S C E N D A N T S R
A G F N R G T M E I M E
N E O F E K N I T G N A
O T S R I F A L A E V E
L A G U T W T Y S N O G
J B N I U L E B A O I S
Y L R T A C R N D C F E
M E T H U S E L A H E T
L S H N I A C I M T L H
```

Quiz 2
GOD STARTS OVER

In the book of Genesis, we read that the people on earth became very bad. Their sinful ways made God sorry that He had created them! So He decided to send a flood to wipe everything away and start over. But God spared Noah and his family.

CAN YOU ANSWER THE FOLLOWING QUESTIONS ABOUT NOAH AND HIS DESCENDANTS?
Use your Bible if you need to.

1. **Why did God save Noah from the flood? (Genesis 6:9)**
   a) because he was a righteous man who walked with God
   b) because he loved animals
   c) because he had a lot of money
   d) because he knew how to build boats

2. **What were the names of Noah's sons? (Genesis 6:10)**
   a) Abraham, Isaac, and Jacob
   b) Shem, Ham, and Japheth
   c) Amos, Obadiah, and Micah
   d) Saul, Jonathan, and David

3. **What did God tell Noah to do to stay safe during the flood? (Genesis 6:14)**
   a) go to an island
   b) climb a high mountain
   c) build an ark
   d) wear a life jacket

4. **What was God's command to Noah when the flood was over? (Genesis 9:7)**
   a) "clean up the mess"
   b) "have many children and fill the earth with people"
   c) "grow lots of food"
   d) "remember the Sabbath day"

5. **What promise did God make to Noah's descendant Abram? (Genesis 12:2)**
   a) he would become a king
   b) he would not have to build a boat
   c) his family would become a great nation
   d) he would own a vineyard

6. **What did Abram do that made God happy? (Genesis 15:6)**
   a) he sang a praise song
   b) he built a temple
   c) he sacrificed a lot of animals
   d) he believed what God said

7. **When God changed Abram's name to Abraham, what did He rename Abraham's wife? (Genesis 17:15)**
   a) Sarah
   b) Rebecca
   c) Leah
   d) Mary

8. **What was the name of the child Abraham and his wife had in their old age? (Genesis 21:3)**
   a) Joseph
   b) Levi
   c) Isaac
   d) Esau

FIND THE MATCH

Draw a line between the arks that are exactly alike.

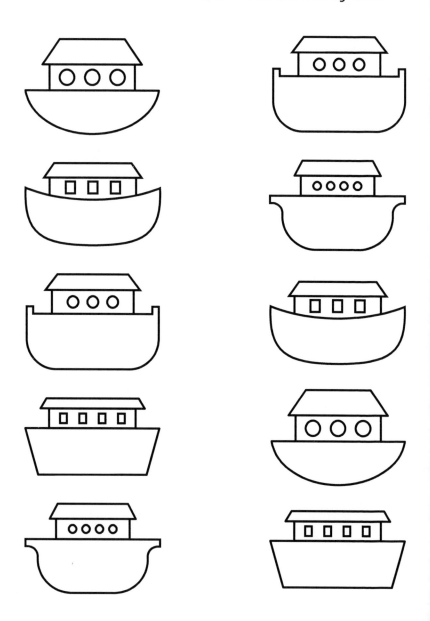

Find the answers on page 142

WORD SEARCH
Can you find all the words?
Words may be forward, backward, or up-and-down.

NOAH	ABRAHAM	FLOOD
SARAH	ARK	JAPHETH
OLD	HAM	PROMISE
SHEM	ISAAC	NAME

```
        H D S M N O A H K L O S H
        M E H S C G M S C D G R A
        F L O O D H T G H K D E M
M B N B M E W D J A P H E T H Q W K B X Z
A R Q K M W B P R O M I S E K B R D L O H
R H D G R T I S A A C B N M S C S A R A H
K B D Q D L L P A B R A H A M T P L X N T
K H G N N A M E T K L P G H R T K F G R E
```

Find the answers on page 142

CROSSWORD PUZZLE

ACROSS

3. The first book of the Bible
5. Noah had three _____ (Genesis 6:10)
7. Abram's new name (Genesis 17:5)
9. The opposite of young
11. The name of Abraham's wife (Genesis 17:15)
12. Another word for trust (Acts 16:31)

DOWN

1. God sent the flood because the people were _____
2. Whom did God see as a righteous man? (Genesis 6:9)
4. The name of Abraham and Sarah's son (Genesis 21:3)
6. God made a _____ to Abraham
8. God told Noah to bring animals into the _____
   (Genesis 7:1–2)
10. One of Noah's sons (Genesis 6:10)

Find the answers on page 142

Quiz 3
THE CHOSEN PEOPLE

God kept His promise to Abraham by giving him a son. Abraham was about a hundred years old and his wife, Sarah, was around ninety! God's promise to Abraham continued through Isaac's family after he got married and had two sons. Isaac's sons were very different from each other and didn't get along well.

WHAT DO YOU KNOW
ABOUT ISAAC AND HIS FAMILY?
You can use your Bible to help you find the answers.

1. **How did God test Abraham's obedience in the land of Moriah? (Genesis 22:2)**
   a) He told Abraham to jump into the Dead Sea
   b) He told Abraham to write Genesis
   c) He told Abraham to marry Hagar
   d) He told Abraham to sacrifice his son

2. **Who did Isaac marry? (Genesis 24:51)**
   a) Rachel
   b) Rebekah
   c) Ruth
   d) Rahab

3. **What were the names of Isaac's twin sons? (Genesis 25:25–26)**
   a) David and Jonathan
   b) Ham and Shem
   c) James and John
   d) Jacob and Esau

4. **How did Jacob trick his father into blessing him? (Genesis 27:18–19)**
   a) he pretended to be his brother, Esau
   b) he switched the lambs of his father's flock with the lambs of his uncle's flock
   c) he asked for his father's blessing while his father was sleeping
   d) he gave his father an expensive gift

5. **Who did Jacob live with when he ran away from Esau? (Genesis 28:5)**
   a) the king
   b) a friend
   c) his grandfather
   d) an uncle

6. **What did God promise Jacob when he left home? (Genesis 28:13)**
   a) he would lead God's people out of Egypt
   b) he would receive a special land for his family
   c) he would have twelve sons
   d) he would become a great prophet

7. **What kind of animals did Jacob's uncle Laban raise? (Genesis 29:9–10)**
   a) cows
   b) pigs
   c) sheep
   d) chickens

8. **What was the name of Laban's daughter who Jacob met at a well? (Genesis 29:10)**
   a) Leah
   b) Deborah
   c) Rachel
   d) Miriam

Find the answers on page 143

SPOT THE DIFFERENCE
Circle the one sheep that is
different from the rest of the flock.

Find the answers on page 143

WORD SEARCH
Can you find all the words?
Words may be forward, backward, or up-and-down.

JACOB	WELL	TWINS
ESAU	PROMISE	REBEKAH
LABAN	STEW	TRICK
SHEEP	ISAAC	LADDER

```
Q R S T E W R P S D C B D T R S
R E B T R K L A D D E R S R E H
L L E W J A C V E S A U G I W E
P R O M I S E L A B W G S C Q E
K S N I W T P I S A A C M K M P
R E B E K A H N P S M A C O B Q
P R H L A B A N S E N J A C O B
```

Find the answers on page 143

CROSSWORD PUZZLE

ACROSS

1. The food Jacob used to cheat Esau (Genesis 25:29)
4. The name Jacob gave the place where he built a pillar to God (Genesis 28:18–19)
5. The name of Jacob's uncle (Genesis 24:29)
7. Jacob stole Esau's _____ (Genesis 27:30–31)
8. Jacob's uncle lived in _____ Aram (Genesis 28:2)
10. Rebekah's husband (Genesis 24:67)
11. Jacob and Esau were _____ (Genesis 25:24–26)

DOWN

1. Rachel's job (Genesis 29:9 NKJV)
2. The place where Jacob met Rachel (Genesis 29:10)
3. God promised to give _____ to Jacob's family (Genesis 28:13)
6. What Jacob saw going up and down a ladder in his dream (Genesis 28:12)
9. Esau's body was very _____ (Genesis 25:25)

Find the answers on page 143

Quiz 4
JACOB GETS MARRIED

God's promise to Abraham continued through Jacob, who was Abraham's grandson. Jacob agreed to work for seven years so he could marry his Uncle Laban's daughter Rachel, whom he loved very much. But Laban tricked Jacob.

LET'S SEE HOW MANY QUESTIONS YOU CAN ANSWER ABOUT JACOB AND HIS FAMILY.
You can use your Bible to look up the references!

1. **What was the trick that Laban played on Jacob? (Genesis 29:25)**
   a) he fooled Jacob into marrying Rachel's sister, Leah
   b) he made Jacob pay 30 pieces of silver
   c) he told Jacob Rachel was sick
   d) he sent Rachel away

2. **What happened to Rachel?**
   (Genesis 29:26–28)
   a) she became Leah's servant
   b) she married the king of the land
   c) she became Jacob's second wife
   d) she moved to China

3. **What new name did God give Jacob?**
   (Genesis 32:28)
   a) Isaac
   b) Isaiah
   c) Ishmael
   d) Israel

4. **How many sons did Jacob have?**
   (Genesis 35:23–26)
   a) 7
   b) 10
   c) 12
   d) 13

5. **What were the names of Rachel's two**
   sons? (Genesis 35:24)
   a) Judah and Manasseh
   b) Joseph and Benjamin
   c) Levi and Simeon
   d) Issachar and Reuben

6. **Why didn't Joseph's brothers like him? (Genesis 37:4)**
   a) he stole their sheep
   b) he ate their dinner
   c) their father liked Joseph the best
   d) their sisters were nice to Joseph

7. **What did Joseph's brothers do to him? (Genesis 37:25-27)**
   a) they stole his sandals
   b) they sold him as a slave
   c) they took his lunch
   d) they shaved his head

8. **What happened when Joseph was in Egypt? (Genesis 41:40)**
   a) he was forced to build the pyramids
   b) he led God's people out of the land
   c) he became the second most important leader
   d) he was in prison for the rest of his life

Find the answers on page 144

COLOR BY NUMBER

Color Joseph's robe using the key below.

1 = Red   2 = Blue   3 = Green   4 = Orange

5 = Yellow   6 = Purple   7 = Pink   8 = Black

CROSSWORD PUZZLE

Find the answers on page 144

ACROSS

1. Laban's oldest daughter (Genesis 29:16)
3. The name of Rachel's youngest son (Genesis 35:24)
7. Joseph told his brothers that the bad things they did to him God used for ____ (Genesis 50:20)
8. Who came to get food in Egypt and didn't recognize Joseph? (Genesis 42:3)
10. The country where Joseph went after his brothers sent him away (Genesis 37:36)
11. Joseph interpreted dreams for Pharaoh's cupbearer and _____ in prison (Genesis 40:5)
12. The name of Leah's youngest son (Genesis 29:35)

DOWN

2. Joseph saw sheaves of wheat, the sun, the moon, and _____ stars bow down in his dreams (Genesis 37:5–9)
4. What was Israel's name before God changed it? (Genesis 35:10)
5. The fancy piece of clothing Joseph's father gave him (Genesis 37:3)
6. Jacob asked Laban for all the speckled and _____ sheep (Genesis 30:31–32)
9. The name of Jacob's firstborn son (Genesis 35:23)

Find the answers on page 144

WORD SEARCH
Can you find all the words?
Words may be forward, backward, or up-and-down.

JOSEPH   PRISON   STARS
TWELVE   WIFE   REUBEN
ROBE   ISRAEL   LEAH
DREAM   BROTHERS   BENJAMIN

```
        A J V W K L E R G D
        Q S U Y L C M I H R S P
        S R T H G K L P T N B T S Q
        S R A T S G R N B E N J A M I N
      F N T L T W E L V E W F H A E L T P
    D R E B T R E U B E N S M Q M E T N T B
    G O T R D R E A M L T J N N D H N J W C
    Q B R O T H E R S H L T V S W B K L I W
    B E K L H P E S O J M W N T K N L S F R
      M P R I S O N T N N S R D H D N K E
        R S R K B I S R A E L W R P K M
        R R Y T J H F J T L B W N S
          T M U I L Z U Q M G A B
          V R A C B H Y F K O
```

Find the answers on page 144

THE ISRAELITES GO TO EGYPT

A famine sent Jacob's sons to Egypt, where they were very surprised to meet Joseph! He forgave his brothers for selling him as a slave, and soon the whole family moved to Egypt. The descendants of Abraham, Isaac, and Jacob were called the Israelites.

WHAT DO YOU KNOW ABOUT THE ISRAELITES AND WHAT HAPPENED TO THEM IN EGYPT?

You can look up the references
in your Bible if you need help.

1. **What did Joseph tell his brothers after their father, Jacob, died? (Genesis 50:21)**
   a) he would send them back home
   b) he would put them in prison
   c) he would provide for them and their children
   d) he would teach them how to make pyramids

2. As time went on after Joseph died, what happened to the Israelites? (Exodus 1:9)
   a) they played too many video games
   b) they moved to Assyria
   c) they grew in number
   d) they invented writing

3. What did the new Egyptian king, the Pharaoh, do to the Israelites? (Exodus 1:14)
   a) he gave them food and sent them back to Canaan
   b) he treated them badly and made them work very hard
   c) he teased them and called them bad names
   d) he made them eat frogs and lizards

4. What did God tell Moses to do? (Exodus 3:10)
   a) become the next Pharaoh of Egypt
   b) build houses for the Israelites
   c) bring the Israelites out of Egypt
   d) climb a pyramid

5. After God sent ten plagues and Pharaoh finally let the Israelites leave Egypt, what body of water did they have to cross? (Exodus 13:18)
   a) the Dead Sea
   b) the Black Sea
   c) the Red Sea
   d) the Deep Blue Sea

6. At the sea, what did God tell Moses to do?
(Exodus 14:15–16)
   a) get into a big boat
   b) start swimming
   c) scream and shout
   d) hold his staff over the sea to divide
   the water

7. What was the first of the Ten
Commandments God gave to Moses and
the Israelites during their wilderness
wandering? (Exodus 20:1–17).
   a) "You shall not talk in the library"
   b) "You shall have no other gods before me"
   c) "You shall not murder"
   d) "Honor your father and your mother"

8. Who became the leader of the Israelites
after Moses? (Deuteronomy 34:9)
   a) Benjamin
   b) Caleb
   c) Joshua
   d) Judah

Find the answers on page 145

CROSSWORD PUZZLE

ACROSS

2. The name of Joseph's father (Genesis 46:19)
3. What moms and dads have
6. The people walked through the sea on _____ ground (Exodus 14:22)
7. The country where Potiphar bought Joseph as a slave (Genesis 39:1)
10. The Israelites lived in the wilderness for forty _____ (Joshua 5:6)
11. Who led the Israelites out of Egypt? (Exodus 14:1–4)

DOWN

1. The Egyptians made the Israelites _____ very hard (Exodus 1:14)
2. The name of Rachel's oldest son (Genesis 35:24)
4. The name that was given to Abraham, Isaac, and Jacob's descendants (Exodus 1:7)
5. What the Israelites had to cross after leaving Egypt (Exodus 13:18)
8. The name given to the king of Egypt (Genesis 39:1)
9. How many commandments did God give to Moses? (Exodus 20:1–17)

Find the answers on page 145

FINISH THE PICTURE

Using the grid provided, draw the reflection of the image shown to complete the picture.

WORD SEARCH
Can you find all the words?
Words may be forward, backward, or diagonal.

PHARAOH   JOSEPH   JACOB
WILDERNESS   MOSES   ISRAELITES
EGYPTIANS   RED SEA   FORTY
COMMANDMENTS   EXODUS   LEADER

```
K H M J Q Z C O M M A N D M E N T S
B O C A J M W N H F O R T Y N H G T
S G F H R M W Q R E D S E A Q R B T
H P E S O J S M T D T R E D A E L M
P Q N K P H A R A O H T S S B X N H
S D I S R A E L I T E S D W F S M Q
H E G Y P T I A N S N Q E X O D U S
C H R W I L D E R N E S S M H N O Q
```

Quiz 6
MORE LEADERS FOR THE ISRAELITES

After Moses died, God used other men and women to lead His people. Joshua led the Israelites across the Jordan River into the land God promised them. Later, God gave other people important jobs as **judges**, a word which can mean "deliverer."

WHAT DO YOU KNOW ABOUT SOME OF ISRAEL'S LEADERS?
If you need help, look up the references in your Bible!

1. What did God tell the priests to do at the Jordan River? (Joshua 3:8)
  a) strike the water with their staffs
  b) stand still in the middle of the river with the ark of the covenant
  c) take off their sandals
  d) throw out their fishing nets

2. **Who went to see Joshua before he went into battle?** (Joshua 5:13–14)
   a) Moses
   b) Jacob's twelve sons
   c) his older brothers
   d) the commander of the Lord's army

3. **What did Joshua and the Israelites do to bring down the wall around Jericho?** (Joshua 6:15, 20)
   a) they fired cannon balls
   b) they knocked it down one stone at a time
   c) they marched around the city seven times, blew their trumpets, and shouted
   d) they poured olive oil over it

4. **Why did the Israelites go to see Deborah?** (Judges 4:4–5)
   a) she sold clothing
   b) she made bread
   c) she taught the people how to sing
   d) she helped to settle the Israelites' disagreements

5. **Who did the Israelites defeat with Deborah's help? (Judges 4:24)**
   a) the king of Canaan
   b) the king of Egypt
   c) the king of Assyria
   d) the king of Midian

6. **What did the angel of the Lord tell Gideon to do? (Judges 6:14)**
   a) tell the Israelites to turn away from their sin
   b) build the temple in Jerusalem
   c) save Israel from the Midianites
   d) lead the Israelites back to Egypt

7. **Why did Gideon think he wasn't good enough to do what the angel said? (Judges 6:15)**
   a) his family was weak and he was the least important family member
   b) he had leprosy and was too sick
   c) he wasn't good at public speaking
   d) he was poor

8. **How many men ended up fighting in Gideon's army? (Judges 7:8)**
   a) 100
   b) 300
   c) 10,000
   d) 22,000

Find the answers on page 146

CONNECT THE DOTS

Starting with number 1, draw a line
to each number in order to create a picture.

CROSSWORD PUZZLE

ACROSS

3. God told Joshua to have twelve men pick up _____ from the river (Joshua 4:2–3)
6. The woman who was saved in Jericho because she helped the spies (Joshua 6:23)
8. The first time Gideon asked God for a sign, God put _____ on the wool but the ground was dry (Judges 6:37)
11. Gideon knew that the _____ was the real leader of Israel (Judges 8:23)
12. The Israelites _____ around the city of Jericho for seven days (Joshua 6:3–4)

DOWN

1. The first time God made Gideon's army smaller, he had ten _____ men who remained (Judges 7:3)
2. The number of times the Israelites marched around Jericho on each of the first six days (Joshua 6:3)
4. Before Joshua died, he said that he and his family would _____ the Lord (Joshua 24:15)
5. Deborah and a commander named Barak _____ to praise God after their victory (Judges 5:1)
7. Deborah was a _____ (Judges 4:4 NKJV)
9. The region where Deborah served as a judge (Judges 4:5)
10. Gideon broke down an _____ to a false god (Judges 6:28)

Find the answers on page 146

WORD SEARCH

Can you find all the words?
Words may be forward, backward, or up-and-down.

JOSHUA	ARMY	MIDIAN
TRUMPET	GIDEON	JORDAN
WALL	RIVER	JUDGE
CANAAN	JERICHO	DEBORAH

```
P T T R U M P E T H D E B B H O D D
J T R H K D E B O R A H N R D S G B
O J O H C I R E J H M W A L L D B A
S B V I Y C A N A A N K L H N R N R
H C N T R I V E R W F R N B K D G M
U X S R E G D U J B D G H R S W C Y
A B N D M I D I A N B R V R W A Q T
N M K T G I D E O N T N A D R O J W
```

Find the answers on page 146

Quiz 7
MOTHERS, DAUGHTERS, AND SONS

The number of Israelites kept getting bigger and bigger. Some of them married people from other countries, but God used these people as part of His plan. A woman named Ruth was one of them. The Bible also tells about an Israelite woman named Hannah who prayed to God for a son. That son became the last judge of Israel.

WHAT DO YOU KNOW ABOUT RUTH AND HANNAH AND THEIR FAMILIES?
Look up the Bible verses if you need help.

1. Why did Naomi and her husband, Elimelech, go to Moab? (Ruth 1:1–2)
   a) to find their relatives
   b) to avoid a famine in Judah
   c) to see the king
   d) to take a vacation

2. Who was Ruth? (Ruth 1:3–4)
a) Naomi's servant
b) Naomi's sister
c) Naomi's daughter-in-law
d) Naomi's cousin

3. What man was kind to Ruth after her husband died? (Ruth 2:8–9)
a) Jacob
b) Moses
c) Joshua
d) Boaz

4. Who was one of Ruth's great-grandsons? (Ruth 4:16–17)
a) David
b) John
c) Peter
d) James

5. What promise did Hannah give to God? (1 Samuel 1:11)
a) to work in the temple
b) to help the poor
c) that if God gave her a son, she would give him back to God
d) to cook meals for the priest

6. What did Hannah name her son?
(1 Samuel 1:20)
- **a)** Samuel
- **b)** Benjamin
- **c)** Jonathan
- **d)** Eli

7. Who spoke to Samuel one night?
(1 Samuel 3:10)
- **a)** a prophet
- **b)** the Lord
- **c)** a king
- **d)** a teacher

8. How long did Samuel lead the people?
(1 Samuel 7:15)
- **a)** until he was twenty-five
- **b)** until he got married
- **c)** until he became a father
- **d)** for his whole life

Find the answers on page 147

CROSSWORD PUZZLE

ACROSS

2. Hannah asked God to give her a _____ (1 Samuel 1:11)
4. Who owned the field where Ruth gathered grain? (Ruth 2:3)
6. Who was Hannah's husband? (1 Samuel 1:1–2)
7. What was the name of the priest who saw Hannah pray? (1 Samuel 1:12)
9. Where did Naomi's family go because of a famine? (Ruth 1:1–2)
10. Whom did Samuel anoint to be the first king of Israel? (1 Samuel 10:1)
11. The Israelites told Samuel they wanted a _____ (1 Samuel 8:5)

DOWN

1. How many sons did Samuel have? (1 Samuel 8:2)
3. Who was Ruth's sister-in-law? (Ruth 1:4)
4. What town was Naomi's family from? (Ruth 1:1)
5. Hannah told the Lord that there is no one _____ like He is (1 Samuel 2:2)
8. What was the name of Naomi's first son? (Ruth 1:2)

Find the answers on page 147

CODED MESSAGE

Use the key below to match the symbols
and fill in the missing letters.

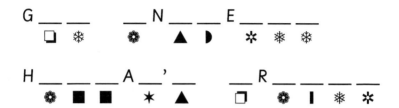

G _ _   _ N _ _ E _ _ _

H _ _ _ A _ ' _   _ R _ _ _ _

Find the answers on page 147

WORD SEARCH
Can you find all the words?
Words may be forward, backward, or up-and-down.

SAMUEL	RUTH	NAOMI
MOAB	FAMINE	ELI
ELKANAH	HANNAH	BOAZ
GRAIN	FIELD	ORPAH

```
G H K L H A N N A H R R D H T U R
R D S A M U E L G R N M D N D K T
A B F Q G R M E L K A N A H M P E
I M B O R P A H M N N A O M I W L
N S D Q F A M I N E W Z D O B Q I
B G R F I E L D B D Q G M O A B W
Q N R T T L Z A O B H N H B R D V
```

Find the answers on page 147

THE FIRST KINGS OF ISRAEL

The Israelites wanted a king like the other nations had. God knew this was their way of rejecting Him as their Lord, but He gave the people what they wanted. Saul was the first king of Israel, followed by David and Solomon.

HOW MANY QUESTIONS CAN YOU ANSWER ABOUT THE FIRST THREE KINGS OF ISRAEL?

Look up the references in your Bible if you need help!

1. How old was Saul when he became the king of Israel? (1 Samuel 13:1)
  a) 10
  b) 30
  c) 45
  d) 97

2. How did David help when King Saul was feeling sad? (1 Samuel 16:23 NKJV)
   a) he played his harp
   b) he gave the king a purple robe
   c) he made goat stew
   d) he played checkers with Saul

3. How did David fight the enemy giant Goliath? (1 Samuel 17:49)
   a) he used karate
   b) he used a slingshot and a stone
   c) he used a bow and arrow
   d) he used a club

4. Why was the kingdom of Israel taken away from Saul? (1 Samuel 13:13–14)
   a) he was lazy
   b) he was a bad soldier
   c) he didn't obey God's command
   d) he married a woman from another country

5. How many years did David rule as king? (2 Samuel 5:4)
   a) 10
   b) 20
   c) 30
   d) 40

6. **David wrote over seventy psalms in the Bible—what does he call God in Psalm 23?**
   a) my King
   b) my Ruler
   c) my Shepherd
   d) my Friend

7. **What did Solomon ask God to give him when he became king? (2 Chronicles 1:10)**
   a) gold and silver
   b) sheep and goats
   c) health and strength
   d) wisdom and knowledge

8. **What did King Solomon get to do that his father, David, could not? (1 Chronicles 22:7–9)**
   a) build the temple in Jerusalem
   b) train his army to fight the Philistines
   c) build houses for all the Israelites
   d) perform miracles

Find the answers on page 148

FIND THE MATCH

Draw a line from the crown on the left to
the matching crown on the right.

Find the answers on page 148

CROSSWORD PUZZLE

ACROSS

2. The name of David's son who became king (1 Kings 2:12)
4. Who was Solomon's mother? (1 Kings 2:13)
5. In what book of the Bible can we find David's songs and prayers?
7. One of the weapons Goliath carried against David (1 Samuel 17:45)
8. Who was David's father? (1 Samuel 17:17)
10. Who anointed David's head with oil? (1 Samuel 16:13)
11. For how many years was Solomon the king of Israel? (1 Kings 11:42)

DOWN

1. Who was David's best friend? (1 Samuel 18:1)
3. Saul was _____ than other people (1 Samuel 9:2)
6. How many brothers did David have? (1 Samuel 16:10)
7. What David was before he became a king (1 Samuel 16:11)
9. The name of Jonathan's father (1 Samuel 14:1)

Find the answers on page 148

WORD SEARCH

Can you find all the words?
Words may be forward, backward, or up-and-down.

KING	SOLOMON	SAUL
GOLIATH	SHEPHERD	DAVID
HARP	ISRAEL	TEMPLE
THRONE	WISDOM	SLINGSHOT

```
J S L I N G S H O T R H
K H S K B W A S J D K G
T E M P L E U A H G I M
M P M W S O L O M O N S
B H A R P A T F L L G A
H E R M W M O D S I W M
F R P A K V I S R A E L
G D I V A D J E V T H T
T H R O N E M A C H B E
```

Find the answers on page 148

Quiz 9
TWO PROPHETS AND A QUEEN

Some of the kings of Israel didn't love God and did evil things. Some of the other leaders were mean to God's people. God chose ordinary people to do some amazing things to help His people during these times.

LET'S SEE HOW MANY QUESTIONS YOU CAN ANSWER ABOUT ELIJAH, ELISHA, AND ESTHER.
Look up the verses in your Bible if you want help.

1. **After Elijah prayed for the rain to stop, how much time passed before it rained again? (James 5:17)**
   a) 2 years
   b) 3 years 6 months
   c) 7 years
   d) 12 years 9 months

2. Which king did Elijah challenge on Mount Carmel? (1 Kings 18:20–21)
   a) Nebuchadnezzar
   b) Herod
   c) Xerxes
   d) Ahab

3. What happened when Elijah was taken to heaven? (2 Kings 2:11)
   a) ravens came to take him away
   b) there was an earthquake in Jerusalem
   c) a chariot of fire and horses appeared
   d) the sun stood still for six hours

4. Whose coat did Elisha take when the time came for him to be a prophet? (2 Kings 2:13)
   a) Ephraim's
   b) Ezekiel's
   c) Elijah's
   d) Eli's

5. What miracle did God have Elisha perform for Naaman? (2 Kings 5:1, 10)
   a) heal him of leprosy
   b) help him walk again
   c) give him back his sight after he became blind
   d) grow hair on his bald head

6. **Who did Elisha secretly anoint as king to replace Ahab? (2 Kings 9:1–3)**
   a) Josiah
   b) David
   c) Saul
   d) Jehu

7. **When Mordecai came to visit Queen Esther, what did he tell her Haman wanted to do to the Jews? (Esther 4:7–8)**
   a) give them each a bag of gold
   b) destroy them
   c) turn them into slaves
   d) send them all to Jerusalem

8. **What secret had Esther kept from King Xerxes? (Esther 2:10)**
   a) she was already married
   b) she was Jewish
   c) she had bribed one of his officers
   d) she wouldn't give honor to Haman

Find the answers on page 149

CROSSWORD PUZZLE

ACROSS

4. The number of months Esther had to do beauty treatments before she could meet King Xerxes (Esther 2:12)
5. God sent an _____ to help Elijah when he ran away to Horeb (1 Kings 19:5)
6. Mordecai treated Esther as his own _____ (Esther 2:7)
7. God used Elisha to raise a woman's _____ from the dead (2 Kings 4:36–37)
11. Esther told Mordecai she could only see the king if he held out his golden _____ (Esther 4:11)

DOWN

1. Elijah told a widow that God would do a miracle and give her enough _____ and oil until the rain came back (1 Kings 17:14)
2. What animals did God send to feed Elijah? (1 Kings 17:2–4)
3. The number of times Elisha told Naaman to wash in the river (2 Kings 5:10)
6. Elisha asked Elijah to give him a _____ share of his spirit (2 Kings 2:9)
8. Elisha did a miracle by helping a widow fill jars with this kind of oil (2 Kings 4:2)
9. The queen Esther replaced (Esther 1:19)
10. God sent _____ to Elijah's altar when he challenged the prophets of Baal (1 Kings 18:38)

Find the answers on page 149

Make as many words as you
can out of the letters in

MORDECAI

_____   _____

_____   _____

_____   _____

_____   _____

_____   _____

_____   _____

_____   _____

_____   _____

_____   _____

WORD SEARCH
Can you find all the words?
Words may be forward, backward, or up-and-down.

ALTAR   SCEPTER   NAMAAN
OIL   RAVENS   XERXES
DOUBLE   JAR   FIRE
QUEEN   MORDECAI   AHAB

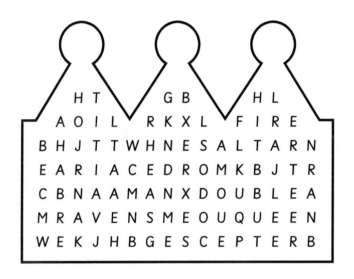

```
    H T       G B       H L
    A O I L   R K X L   F I R E
B H J T T W H N E S A L T A R N
E A R I A C E D R O M K B J T R
C B N A A M A N X D O U B L E A
M R A V E N S M E O U Q U E E N
W E K J H B G E S C E P T E R B
```

Quiz 10
MORE PROPHETS

God's people started to love other things more than they loved Him. God sent prophets to warn the people that they needed to return to Him in love.

WHAT DO YOU KNOW
ABOUT SOME OF GOD'S PROPHETS?
Look up the references in your Bible if you need to.

1. **Why is Jeremiah's nickname "the weeping prophet"? (Jeremiah 9:1)**
   a) he was happy to see the temple finished
   b) he was sad about what was going happen to the Israelites
   c) he had allergies and his eyes watered
   d) he was blind

2. Why did Jeremiah think he wasn't good enough to be God's prophet? (Jeremiah 1:6)
   a) he was young and didn't speak well
   b) he was poor
   c) the Israelites didn't like him
   d) he had no children to follow his footsteps

3. Whose house did God use to give Jeremiah a message for the people? (Jeremiah 18:1-2)
   a) a doctor's
   b) a teacher's
   c) a baker's
   d) a potter's

4. What name did the Babylonians give to Daniel? (Daniel 1:7)
   a) Shadrach
   b) Belteshazzar
   c) Meshach
   d) Abednego

5. What promise did Daniel keep so that he wouldn't break God's rules? (Daniel 1:8)
   a) he walked into town instead of riding a horse
   b) he melted all of his gold so it couldn't be turned into an idol
   c) he wouldn't take the king's food or wine
   d) he didn't speak so he wouldn't tell a lie

6. Why was Daniel thrown into the lions' den? (Daniel 6:10)

a) he wouldn't bow down to the statue of the king

b) his brothers were jealous that he had become an important helper to the king

c) he prayed to God three times a day even though it was against the king's law

d) his friend told a lie and said that Daniel had stolen the king's gold cup

7. Which city did God tell Jonah to go to? (Jonah 1:1–2)

a) Bethlehem

b) Tarshish

c) Nazareth

d) Nineveh

8. How long was Jonah in the belly of a huge fish? (Jonah 1:17)

a) three days and three nights

b) seven days

c) twelve days and twelve nights

d) forty days

Find the answers on page 150

MATCH THE PROPHET TO HIS STORY

Draw a line from the names of the prophets on the left to the related picture on the right. Be careful—there are two extra pictures that don't match!

JEREMIAH

DANIEL

JONAH

Find the answers on page 150

CROSSWORD PUZZLE

ACROSS

3. Who did God send to shut the lions' mouths so Daniel would be safe? (Daniel 6:22)
5. God said that Israel was like clay and He was like a _____ (Jeremiah 18:5–6)
7. Where did Jonah go when God told him to go to Nineveh? (Jonah 1:3)
11. God commanded the fish to spit Jonah out on dry ____ (Jonah 2:10)
12. God chose Jeremiah to be a _____ to the nations (Jeremiah 1:5)

DOWN

1. God helped Daniel read the writing on the ____ that no one else could understand (Daniel 5:5)
2. Where did the Israelites go when they didn't listen to the message God gave Jeremiah? (Jeremiah 43:6–7)
4. Whose dream did Daniel explain? (Daniel 2:28)
6. The place Daniel lived after the Israelites were defeated (Daniel 1:1)
8. What was wrapped around Jonah's head while he was in the belly of the fish? (Jonah 2:5)
9. God told Jeremiah to write the words He spoke on a _____ (Jeremiah 36:1–2)
10. The people of Nineveh _____ God's warning (Jonah 3:5)

Find the answers on page 150

WORD SEARCH
Can you find all the words?
Words may be forward, backward, or up-and-down.

JEREMIAH	POTTER	SCROLL
NINEVEH	WEEPING	LIONS
DANIEL	FISH	TARSHISH
JONAH	PRAY	MOUTH

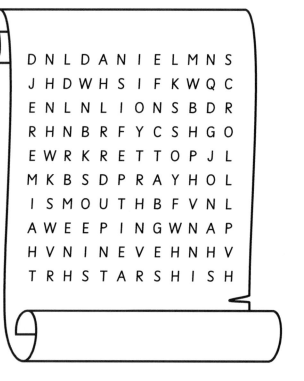

D N L D A N I E L M N S
J H D W H S I F K W Q C
E N L N L I O N S B D R
R H N B R F Y C S H G O
E W R K R E T T O P J L
M K B S D P R A Y H O L
I S M O U T H B F V N L
A W E E P I N G W N A P
H V N I N E V E H N H V
T R H S T A R S H I S H

Find the answers on page 150

Quiz 11
A SAVIOR FOR THE PEOPLE

The Israelites had turned away from God many times. They were led by judges, prophets, and kings. But now it was time for God to fulfill His promise to give them a Savior—someone who could forgive their sins and make them holy before Him. The Savior's name is Jesus.

WHAT DO YOU KNOW ABOUT JESUS, HIS PARENTS, AND HIS BIRTH?
Use your Bible if you need help!

1. **What did the angel Gabriel say to a young woman named Mary? (Luke 1:28)**
   a) "Go to Bethlehem."
   b) "You are going to be famous."
   c) "The Lord is with you."
   d) "You will have many children."

2. How did Mary respond when Gabriel told her she would be the mother of God's Son? (Luke 1:38)

a) "I am the Lord's servant."
b) "I am too young."
c) "I am not married."
d) "I have other plans."

3. What did Joseph do after an angel spoke to him in a dream? (Matthew 1:24)

a) he ran away
b) he broke up with Mary
c) he married Mary
d) he gave Mary a gold ring

4. Where was Joseph's family from? (Luke 2:4)

a) Nazareth
b) Bethany
c) Bethlehem
d) Canaan

5. Why were some shepherds afraid the night Jesus was born? (Luke 2:9)

a) they lost their sheep
b) they saw a wolf
c) they heard a loud noise
d) a bright angel stood before them

6. **What did the shepherds do when they heard that Jesus had been born? (Luke 2:16–18)**
   a) they went to church and sang praise songs
   b) they ran to find Jesus, then told everyone what had happened
   c) they fell asleep because they were tired
   d) they brought gifts of gold and frankincense to Jesus

7. **Who held Jesus when Mary and Joseph brought him to the temple? (Luke 2:25–28)**
   a) Simeon
   b) Simon
   c) Solomon
   d) Saul

8. **Why did the prophetess Anna get to see Jesus? (Luke 2:36–38)**
   a) she was Joseph's cousin
   b) she was Mary's sister
   c) the shepherds told her to go to the temple
   d) she was always at the temple

Find the answers on page 151

CROSSWORD PUZZLE

ACROSS

1. The angel told Mary her baby would be called the Son of
   _____ (Luke 1:35)
3. The name of Jesus's earthly father (Luke 2:22)
5. An angel spoke to Joseph in a _____ (Matthew 1:20)
6. Who were the first people to visit baby Jesus? (Luke 2:15–17)
10. The name of the angel who visited Mary (Luke 1:26–27)
11. What was the name of the man who baptized Jesus?
    (Matthew 3:13)

DOWN

1. The angel told Mary that Jesus would be _____ (Luke 1:32)
2. What insects did John the Baptist eat? (Matthew 3:4)
4. Bethlehem was also called the town of _____ (Luke 2:4)
7. The name of Mary's relative who was also going to have a
   baby (Luke 1:36)
8. Who told Simeon he would see the Messiah before he died?
   (Luke 2:26)
9. The town where Mary lived (Luke 1:26–27)

Find the answers on page 151

Help the shepherd get to the manger.

Find the answers on page 151

WORD SEARCH
Can you find all the words?
Words may be forward, backward, or up-and-down.

JESUS	JOHN	ELIZABETH
ANNA	MESSIAH	SIMEON
ANGEL	JOSEPH	GABRIEL
MARY	SHEEP	SHEPHERDS

```
K D S H E P H E R D S H M H B J
M H P P G K M P E E H S K R L O
A B R L T G A B R I E L M Q G H
R K N H S U S J E S U S W Q D N
Y N B C D L R J T A N N A K L B
K N G L L E G N A V J L N P H R
S M S I M E O N K M J O S E P H
H T E B A Z I L E K Z D Z L W B
M S H S M E S S I A H K L T N D
```

Find the answers on page 151

Quiz 12
THE TWELVE DISCIPLES

Jesus chose twelve men to be His helpers. The "disciples" were ordinary men who followed Jesus during His years of teaching and doing miracles. They did not understand everything He taught them, but they were faithful to help Him while He lived on earth.

WHAT DO YOU KNOW
ABOUT JESUS'S TWELVE DISCIPLES?
The Bible verses will help you find the answers.

1. **What did Jesus say to Simon Peter and his brother Andrew? (Matthew 4:18–19)**
   a) "It's a beautiful morning!"
   b) "Did you catch any fish?"
   c) "Where is your boat?"
   d) "Come, follow me."

2. What were the names of two other brothers that Jesus called to follow Him? (Matthew 4:21)
   a) James and Matthew
   b) John and George
   c) James and John
   d) Peter and Paul

3. Who was not among Jesus's original twelve disciples? (Luke 6:13–16)
   a) Simon Peter
   b) Philip
   c) Bartholomew
   d) Paul

4. What did Jesus tell the disciples when parents brought their children to Him? (Matthew 19:14)
   a) "Send the children away."
   b) "Give them something to eat."
   c) "Let the children come to me."
   d) "It's time for them to sleep."

5. What did Philip ask Jesus to do? (John 14:8)
   a) turn water into wine
   b) show the disciples the Father
   c) heal his mother
   d) make it rain

6. What did Peter do that none of the other disciples did? (Matthew 14:29)

a) turn stones into bread
b) heal ten lepers
c) call Jesus his friend
d) walk on the water

7. What did Peter tell Jesus in Matthew 16:15–16?

a) "You are the Messiah, the Son of the living God."
b) "You are my brother and friend."
c) "You are my leader and teacher."
d) "You are healer and Savior."

8. What bad thing did Judas agree to do? (Luke 22:3–6)

a) break into the temple
b) steal food from the poor
c) turn Jesus over to His enemies
d) give money to Jesus's enemies

Find the answers on page 152

FILL IN THE BLANKS

Fill in the missing letters to list
the names of Jesus's Twelve Disciples.
(Turn to Luke 6:13–16 if you need help.)

S _ M O _   P E _ _ R

A N _ _ E _

J _ M _ _

J _ H _

P _ I _ I _

B A _ T H _ L _ M _ W

M _ T _ H _ _

T _ O _ A _

J A _ _ S
(son of Alphaeus)

S I _ _ N
(called the Zealot)

J _ D _ S
(son of James)

J U _ _ S   I S _ _ R _ _ T

Find the answers on page 152

CROSSWORD PUZZLE

ACROSS

2. How many disciples did Jesus have? (Luke 6:13)
4. Philip, Andrew, and Peter were from what town? (John 1:44)
7. Besides the disciples, many people _____ Jesus (Matthew 4:25)
10. What other name did Jesus call His helpers? (Luke 6:13)
11. Who walked on the water to meet Jesus? (Matthew 14:29)

DOWN

1. Which disciple was a tax collector? (Matthew 9:9)
3. Who was the father of James and John? (Matthew 4:21)
5. Who was Peter's brother? (Matthew 4:18)
6. The name of the sea where Jesus met Simon Peter and Andrew (Matthew 4:18)
7. What were Simon Peter and Andrew doing when Jesus called them? (Matthew 4:18)
8. What did Jesus have at Matthew's house? (Matthew 9:10)
9. Jesus told Philip that anyone who sees Jesus also sees the _____ (John 14:9)

Find the answers on page 152

WORD SEARCH
Can you find all the words?
Words may be forward, backward, or diagonal.

APOSTLES	DISCIPLES	THOMAS
ANDREW	MATTHEW	JOHN
PHILIP	JAMES	FOLLOW
PETER	FISHERMEN	HELPERS

```
A  P  L  R  S  H  E  L  P  E  R  S  H  P  S  G  K  N
N  N  T  P  I  L  I  H  P  M  T  H  F  O  L  L  O  W
R  G  D  K  D  I  S  C  I  P  L  E  S  K  G  Q  H  N
P  L  W  R  K  L  T  J  O  H  N  J  V  R  T  V  B  L
H  E  C  F  E  N  F  S  E  M  A  J  K  T  N  J  P  H
Q  V  T  S  T  W  J  T  T  H  O  M  A  S  J  L  D  F
H  Q  G  E  K  K  N  J  M  A  T  T  H  E  W  N  T  P
Q  R  T  H  R  M  B  F  I  S  H  E  R  M  E  N  J  T
A  P  S  Q  G  W  A  P  O  S  T  L  E  S  M  N  R  F
```

Find the answers on page 152

JESUS PERFORMS MIRACLES FOR THE PEOPLE

Jesus did miracles for all kinds of people. He helped rich people and poor people. He used both young and old people to show God's glory through His miracles. He didn't look at the things most people see from the outside. Jesus cared about people's hearts.

HERE ARE SOME QUESTIONS ABOUT A FEW OF THE PEOPLE IN JESUS'S MIRACLES.

How many questions can you answer?

1. Who did Jairus ask Jesus to heal?
   (Luke 8:42)
   a) his daughter
   b) his son
   c) his mother
   d) his wife

2. What was Jairus's job? (Luke 8:41)
a) tax collector
b) lawyer
c) doctor
d) ruler of a synagogue

3. What did Jesus tell Jairus to do for his request to be answered? (Luke 8:50)
a) offer a sacrifice at the temple
b) believe, and not be afraid
c) pray loudly in the city square
d) memorize the 23rd Psalm

4. Why was Jesus delayed in reaching Jairus's house? (Luke 8:42–48)
a) He raised Lazarus from the dead
b) He changed water into wine at a wedding
c) He healed a woman with a bleeding problem
d) He caught a fish with a coin in its mouth

5. Where was Jesus teaching when a hungry crowd of more than 5,000 surrounded him? (John 6:1)
a) by the Jordan River
b) by the Red Sea
c) by the Sea of Galilee
d) by the Jabbok River

6. **Which disciple told Jesus about a boy with some food?** (John 6:8–9)
   a) Philip
   b) Andrew
   c) Peter
   d) James

7. **What exactly did the boy have?** (John 6:9)
   a) five fish and two loaves
   b) a fish and two loaves
   c) two fish and five loaves
   d) seven fish and seven loaves

8. **How many baskets were left over after Jesus miraculously fed the whole crowd?** (John 6:13)
   a) three
   b) seven
   c) ten
   d) twelve

Find the answers on page 153

CROSSWORD PUZZLE

ACROSS

4. When Jesus went to Jairus's house, only Peter, _____, and John were allowed to go inside with Him (Luke 8:51)
5. The age of Jairus's daughter (Luke 8:42)
7. Which festival were the Jews celebrating when Jesus fed the big crowd? (John 6:4)
9. A woman who came to Jesus was _____ (Luke 8:47)
10. The crowd of 5,000 followed Jesus because they saw Him heal ____ people (John 6:2)

DOWN

1. Jesus asked _____ where they would get enough food to feed the people (John 6:5)
2. When Jairus came to Jesus, he fell down at Jesus's ____ (Luke 8:41)
3. When the disciples picked up the leftovers, they filled twelve _____ (John 6:13)
5. While Jairus was talking to Jesus, a woman came and _____ Jesus's clothes (Luke 8:44)
6. What did Jesus do to the bread after He looked up to heaven? (Luke 9:16)
8. When Jesus healed Jairus's daughter, He told the other people to give her something to ____ (Luke 8:55)
11. After Jesus fed the people, they wanted Him to be their ____ (John 6:15)

Find the answers on page 153

Help take the little boy's lunch to Jesus!

Find the answers on page 153

WORD SEARCH
Can you find all the words?
Words may be forward, backward, or up-and-down.

FISH   HEALER   PASSOVER
BASKETS   ANDREW   PHILIP
THOUSAND   JAIRUS   TWELVE
LOAVES   BELIEVE   FEET

```
L B H E A L E R G H P T H F C T
O T R G H E V L E W T H T E J H
A K B P H I L I P N B C T E N O
V B S K D H S I F T S D W T B U
E S K B A S K E T S H D N B K S
S D T A N D R E W J T I M T H A
B J A I R U S K B Q D N V S T N
R E V O S S A P M N T H T L N D
D S W G H K J L B E L I E V E G
```

Find the answers on page 153

JESUS HEALS PEOPLE

Sick and hurting people became part of Jesus's great story when He showed His power in healing them. These people didn't do anything to earn such blessing—they just believed Jesus could help them. And we still read their stories today!

HOW MUCH DO YOU KNOW ABOUT A DEAF MAN AND A BLIND MAN THAT JESUS HEALED?

Answer the questions below to find out.

1. **What did Jesus do to heal a deaf man who couldn't speak? (Mark 7:33)**
   a) He spit on the ground and placed mud on the man's ears
   b) He put His fingers in the man's ears and touched the man's tongue
   c) He placed one hand on the man's head
   d) He spoke without touching the man at all

2. **Where did Jesus heal the deaf man?**
   (Mark 7:33)
   a) inside the temple
   b) on the Mount of Olives
   c) in private, away from everyone
   d) in front of a large crowd

3. **What did it mean when Jesus said,**
   "Ephphatha"? (Mark 7:34)
   a) "be opened"
   b) "be silent"
   c) "come out"
   d) "be healed"

4. **What did people do when Jesus told them**
   not to tell anyone about the deaf man's
   healing? (Mark 7:36)
   a) they didn't tell anyone
   b) they told the priest but no one else
   c) they sent secret letters to their friends and families
   d) they kept talking about it

5. **Where did Jesus meet blind Bartimaeus?**
   (Mark 10:46)
   a) Nazareth
   b) Jerusalem
   c) Bethlehem
   d) Jericho

6. What did Bartimaeus say to Jesus? (Mark 10:47)

a) "Have mercy on me!"
b) "Behold, the Lamb of God!"
c) "I believe! Help my unbelief!"
d) "Remember me when You come into Your kingdom!"

7. What did Bartimaeus do when the crowd told him to be quiet? (Mark 10:48)

a) he sent a friend to talk to Jesus privately
b) he gave up and went home
c) he called out to Jesus even more
d) he ran after Jesus

8. Why did Jesus say Bartimaeus was healed? (Mark 10:52)

a) he didn't give up
b) he had faith
c) he gave an offering at the temple
d) he followed the Ten Commandments

Find the answers on page 154

CONNECT THE DOTS

Connect the dots below to see a message.

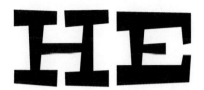

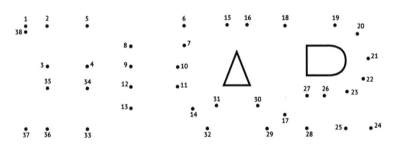

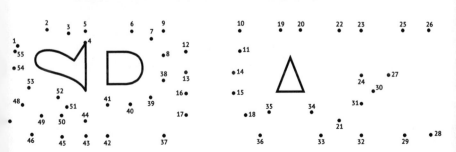

CROSSWORD PUZZLE

ACROSS

2. Bartimaeus threw off his _____ when Jesus called him (Mark 10:50 NIrV)
4. Where did Jesus look to before He healed the deaf man? (Mark 7:34)
6. As soon as Bartimaeus was healed, he _____ Jesus on the road (Mark 10:52)
9. What did Jesus do before He touched the deaf man's tongue? (Mark 7:33)
11. The people who brought the deaf man to Jesus wanted Jesus to lay His _____ on the man (Mark 7:32)
12. Bartimaeus earned money by being a _____ (Mark 10:46)

DOWN

1. What was Bartimaeus sitting by when Jesus passed his way? (Mark 10:46)
3. Where had Jesus come back from when he healed the deaf man? (Mark 7:31)
5. When people saw Jesus heal the deaf man, they said Jesus does _____ well (Mark 7:37)
7. Bartimaeus called Jesus the Son of _____ (Mark 10:47)
8. The deaf man began to _____ clearly as soon as Jesus healed him (Mark 7:35)
10. The name of Bartimaeus's father (Mark 10:46)

Find the answers on page 154

WORD SEARCH
Can you find all the words?
Words may be forward, backward, or diagonal.

BARTIMAEUS   BLIND   YEARS

DEAF   FAITH   TONGUE

SPEAK   JERICHO   CROWD

EPHPHATHA   MERCY   BEGGAR

```
B D F G H F A E D K N S P E A K
N L P N B F S R A E Y F A I T H
B Z I R G H D M E R C Y T H N P
N E T N L P V N C R O W D T L V
K L G H D V F G B T O N G U E L
N B T G V C M O H C I R E J K T
B C R S A W B A R T I M A E U S
G B R T H R N B T H P H T D R N
S D R A H T A H P H P E M N T S
```

JESUS'S SPECIAL FRIENDS

Jesus traveled though many towns and villages to heal people, bless little children, and tell people about God. But some of the people Jesus met became His special friends—like Mary and Martha and their brother Lazarus.

LET'S SEE HOW MANY QUESTIONS YOU CAN ANSWER ABOUT MARY, MARTHA, AND LAZARUS.
Use your Bible if you need help.

1. **What did Mary do when Jesus came to their home? (Luke 10:38–39)**
   a) she made coffee for Jesus
   b) she served Him breakfast
   c) she sat by Jesus and listened to Him
   d) she told Jesus stories

2. What did Martha do while Jesus was at their house? (Luke 10:40)
   a) she sang songs
   b) she was busy working in the house
   c) she played the tambourine
   d) she went outside to pick flowers

3. Where did Mary, Martha, and Lazarus live? (John 11:1)
   a) Bethany
   b) Nazareth
   c) Jerusalem
   d) Samaria

4. What message did Mary and Martha send to Jesus? (John 11:3)
   a) "It's time for dinner"
   b) "Help us find Lazarus"
   c) "We made a robe for you"
   d) "Your friend Lazarus is sick"

5. What happened before Jesus came to their house? (John 11:17)
   a) Lazarus got better
   b) Lazarus got leprosy
   c) Lazarus died
   d) Lazarus went to the hospital

6. **What miracle did Jesus do so the people would believe He was God's Son? (John 11:41–44)**
   a) He rolled the stone away from the tomb
   b) He raised Lazarus from the dead
   c) He made it lightning and thunder
   d) He caused an earthquake

7. **What did Martha do when Jesus came to their house for dinner again? (John 12:2)**
   a) she baked a fig cake for Jesus
   b) she made some grape juice
   c) she served the food
   d) she gave a speech

8. **What did Mary do? (John 12:3)**
   a) she helped Martha bake bread
   b) she poured the juice
   c) she washed the dishes
   d) she poured expensive perfume over Jesus's feet

Find the answers on page 155

CROSSWORD PUZZLE

ACROSS

2. Martha let Jesus stay at her _____ (Luke 10:38)
4. What Jesus did before He called out to Lazarus (John 11:41–42)
6. Who was Mary's sister? (John 11:1)
8. Jesus said that Lazarus's sickness was for God's _____ (John 11:4)
11. What covered the entrance to the tomb where Lazarus was buried? (John 11:38–39)
12. When Lazarus came out of the tomb his body was _____ in strips of cloth (John 11:44)

DOWN

1. Jesus told Martha she was _____ and upset about many things (Luke 10:41)
3. What did Mary pour on Jesus's feet? (John 12:3)
5. Many of Mary's friends who saw what Jesus did _____ in Him (John 11:45)
7. Which disciple wanted to go with Jesus to see Lazarus? (John 11:16)
9. How many days was Lazarus dead before Jesus arrived? (John 11:17)
10. Jesus _____ Mary, Martha, and Lazarus (John 11:5)

Find the answers on page 155

Help Mary and Martha find their way to their good friend Jesus!

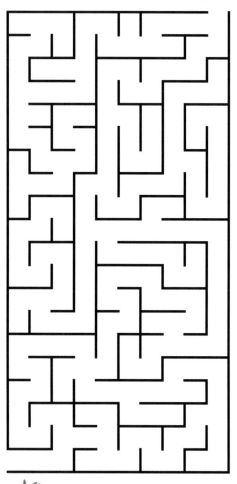

Find the answers on page 155

WORD SEARCH
Can you find all the words?
Words may be forward, backward, or up-and-down.

LAZARUS	FEET	STONE
PERFUME	TOMB	JESUS
BETHANY	MARTHA	HOME
MARY	DINNER	FRIENDS

```
N K N M A R Y T J S
C H O M E S M T E E F S
N M A R T H A D H E N O T B
B M P E R F U M E H D W N O V G
R B E T H A N Y Q W N M R M D K
S T O N E Q B J E S U S H B Q N
D G H D S D N E I R F H N T
L A Z A R U S D Q K N B
R G N R E N N I D M
```

Quiz 16
JESUS AND NICODEMUS

Some Jewish leaders wanted to be saved through obeying the law, but Jesus had a different message. A Jewish leader named Nicodemus knew there was something special about Jesus, and had some questions for Him.

HOW MANY QUESTIONS CAN YOU ANSWER ABOUT NICODEMUS?
The Bible verses will help you find the answers.

1. When did Nicodemus talk to Jesus? (John 3:2)
a) early in the morning
b) at noon
c) at suppertime
d) at night

2. What did Nicodemus already believe about Jesus? (John 3:2)
a) that His mother was Mary
b) that He was sent from God
c) that He could perform miracles
d) that He had many followers

3. What did Jesus tell Nicodemus? (John 3:3)
a) that everyone must be baptized
b) that everyone must become a disciple
c) that everyone must be born again
d) that everyone must go to church

4. How did Nicodemus react to Jesus's words? (John 3:4, 9)
a) he walked away
b) he laughed
c) he became angry
d) he asked questions

5. What did Jesus explain to Nicodemus? (John 3:16)
a) that he had to obey the law to be saved
b) that he had to be a missionary to be saved
c) that he had to believe in Jesus to be saved
d) that he had to read the Bible to be saved

6. Why did God send Jesus into the world? (John 3:16)

a) so Jesus could do miracles
b) so Jesus could heal the sick
c) so Jesus could teach us to be kind
d) because God loves us so much

7. What did Jesus say about the things He taught people? (John 7:16)

a) "My teaching comes from God, who sent Me"
b) "My teaching comes from the law"
c) "My teaching comes from angels"
d) "My teaching comes from a dream"

8. What did Nicodemus say when some of the Jewish leaders wanted to arrest Jesus? (John 7:50–51)

a) "Jesus has done nothing wrong"
b) "Let Jesus go home"
c) "Our law says we must first find out what He has done"
d) "You guys are bullies"

Find the answers on page 156

FILL IN THE BLANKS

See if you can fill in the words to this Bible verse without looking it up. After you finish, check the verse to see if your words are correct.

"For _____ so _____

the world that he _____

his one and only _____ ,

that whoever _____ in him

shall _____ perish but have

_____ _____."

John 3:16 (NIV)

Find the answers on page 156

WORD SEARCH
Can you find all the words?
Words may be forward, backward, or up-and-down.

JESUS	BORN	SAVED
LEADERS	BELIEVE	JEWISH
LOVE	QUESTIONS	NIGHT
NICODEMUS	AGAIN	WORLD

```
H M D G N I C O D E M U S N C M S L
Q R W R L T I G N I G H T Q K L N O
H G S H S I W E J N B T Y N S W T V
P W B E L I E V E M W N R O B H L E
B V N G A G A I N T H S A V E D K L
R S S R E D A E L M W Q S T O N S H
M D L P N S Q U E S T I O N S N G T
B V K L J E S U S N M W O R L D G F
```

Find the answers on page 156

ACROSS

3. For God so loved the _____ (John 3:16)
5. Jesus is the _____ of God (John 3:16)
6. Jesus was with God in the _____ (John 1:2)
8. Another name for Jesus (John 1:1)
9. What can only Jesus give us? (Acts 4:12)
11. Another name given to a Jewish leader (John 3:1)

DOWN

1. We must _____ in Jesus to have eternal life (John 3:15)
2. Nicodemus knew Jesus was sent from ____ (John 3:2)
4. Jesus said we must be born again to be in God's ____ (John 3:3)
5. Jesus said we must be born of water and the ____ (John 3:5)
7. Who is the only way to God the Father? (John 14:6)
10. What word is used to describe Jesus in John 3:19?

Find the answers on page 156

JESUS AND THE CROSS

God sent Jesus to the world to take away our sins. He came not just for the Israelites, but for all people. When He died on the cross, Jesus took the punishment we deserved. If we believe in Him, we can be with God forever.

HERE ARE SOME QUESTIONS ABOUT JESUS'S DEATH AND RESURRECTION.
You can use the Bible verses to help you find the answers.

1. **Where was Jesus praying when Judas brought enemies to arrest Him? (Matthew 26:36)**
   a) the garden of Gethsemane
   b) the temple court
   c) the pool of Siloam
   d) the gate of Jerusalem

2. Who was the Roman governor that Jesus was taken to? (John 18:28–29)
   a) Caesar
   b) Herod
   c) Pilate
   d) Caiaphas

3. What did the governor tell the Jews after he talked to Jesus? (John 18:38)
   a) that Jesus was a criminal
   b) that he found no guilt in Jesus
   c) that Jesus should be crucified
   d) that Jesus should be thrown in prison

4. What did Pilate want to do after ordering Jesus to be beaten? (John 19:12)
   a) put Him in prison
   b) release Him
   c) send Him back to the chief priest
   d) crucify Him

5. What did Pilate have written on a sign that was nailed to Jesus's cross? (John 19:19)
   a) "Behold, the Lamb of God"
   b) "A Criminal from Nazareth"
   c) "Guilty"
   d) "Jesus of Nazareth, the King of the Jews"

6. Which two men buried Jesus after He died? (John 19:38–39)

a) Simon of Cyrene and Judas
b) Peter and John
c) Saul of Tarsus and Barnabas
d) Joseph of Arimathea and Nicodemus

7. Who asked Mary Magdalene why she was crying near Jesus's tomb? (John 20:11–13)

a) two angels
b) Peter and John
c) the gardener
d) Pilate

8. When Mary realized that Jesus had come back from the dead, what did she say to Him? (John 20:15–18)

a) "Hallelujah!"
b) "My Lord!"
c) "Rabboni!" (which means "Teacher!")
d) "You're alive!"

Find the answers on page 157

What was Mary Magdalene's
message to the disciples?
Use the key below to match the symbols
to letters to break the code.

JESUS IS ALIVE!

CROSSWORD PUZZLE

ACROSS

1. The robber Pilate released instead of Jesus (John 18:39–40)
3. When Jesus appeared to the disciples after He rose from the dead, the doors to the room were _____ (John 20:19)
7. The women who followed Joseph to Jesus's tomb were from _____ (Luke 23:55)
9. The disciple who gave Jesus over to His enemies (Luke 22:48)
10. The man who helped Jesus carry His cross (Luke 23:26)
11. The disciple who said he did not know Jesus (John 18:17)

DOWN

2. What was Jesus's tomb made from? (Luke 23:53)
4. Mary Magdalene told the _____ that Jesus rose from the dead (John 20:18)
5. How many pounds of spices did Nicodemus bring to prepare Jesus for burial? (John 19:39)
6. The high priest when Jesus was arrested (John 18:13)
8. Who did Mary think Jesus was when she first saw Him? (John 20:15)
9. Pilate asked Jesus if He was king of the ____ (John 18:33)

Find the answers on page 157

WORD SEARCH
Can you find all the words?
Words may be forward, backward, up-and-down, or diagonal.

PILATE   ANNAS   BARABBAS   TOMB
GARDENER   MARY   GOVERNOR   SIMON
JUDAS   JEWS   ROCK   CAIAPHAS

```
            H G K C O R
            K L B B T W
            D M A R Y G
            R C R L T R
    E T O M B Q U A K E T A L I P U
    X G N S I O R B H M B T W I L M
    M C I H S O W B W L G E R Y K A
    V P R I C A I A P H A S J N I T
    T E O B A I F S E T R U T W S M
    G O V E R N O R Q R D F S H U T
            W N M E N E
            Z A A G E N
            J C R S W E
            U U B W O R
            D G Z A E D
            A O M B R L
            S I M O N G
            Y E P O K N
            D A H K L O
            J U S W E J
            O H N B E C
```

Find the answers on page 157

Quiz 18
THE DISCIPLES TEACH THE FIRST CHRISTIANS

After Jesus went back to heaven, His helpers taught the new Christians about Jesus. The disciples did many great things through the Holy Spirit, and kept following Jesus even when other people tried to stop them.

HOW MUCH DO YOU KNOW ABOUT THE DISCIPLES AND THE FIRST CHRISTIANS?
Answer the questions below to find out!

1. **During what holiday did the Holy Spirit come to earth to live inside Jesus's followers? (Acts 2:1–4)**
   a) Pentecost
   b) Passover
   c) Yom Kippur
   d) Purim

2. Who preached a sermon that led three thousand people to believe in Jesus? (Acts 2:14, 41)
   a) Stephen
   b) Peter
   c) Paul
   d) John

3. Which of the following is not something the early Christians did together? (Acts 2:42)
   a) put up a church building
   b) listen to the apostles' teaching
   c) pray
   d) eat together

4. What happened to Peter and John when the Jewish leaders heard them speaking about Jesus? (Acts 4:3)
   a) they were invited to speak at the temple on the Sabbath
   b) they were beaten with sticks
   c) they were arrested and put in jail
   d) they were sent to Egypt

5. **Why did people lay their sick friends on the streets of Jerusalem? (Acts 5:15)**
   a) so the sun would keep them warm
   b) so they could hear the disciples' preaching
   c) so they could look for angels in the sky
   d) so Peter's shadow might touch them

6. **What wise Pharisee told other Jewish leaders not to kill the apostles? (Acts 5:33–39)**
   a) Gabriel
   b) Gideon
   c) Goliath
   d) Gamaliel

7. **What were the last words spoken by Stephen, the first Christian killed for following Jesus? (Acts 7:60)**
   a) "How dare you?"
   b) "My life is but a breath"
   c) "Lord, do not hold this sin against them"
   d) "It is finished"

8. **Who preached the good news about Jesus in Samaria? (Acts 8:4–5)**
   a) Bartholomew
   b) Philip
   c) Thomas
   d) James

Find the answers on page 158

BACKWARDS MESSAGE

The sentence below is written backward from right to left. Starting with the letter T, rewrite it forward from left to right to reveal a special message.

DEZITPAB EB DNA NIS RUOY MORF NRUT

_____

_____

_____

_____

_____

WORD SEARCH
Can you find all the words?
Words may be forward, backward, up-and-down, or diagonal.

PENTECOST	PORTICO	BELIEVE
HOLY SPIRIT	JAIL	JOHN
PHILIP	SERMON	PETER
STEPHEN	BAPTIZE	GAMALIEL

```
J K L M N B G R E T E P K L B
N O N K J Q H N N P R T Z B A
B C H W T N B L I A J Z K N P
B D N N K T R D H T N C R R T
S H G L M G A M A L I E L G I
B H L H O L Y S P I R I T R Z
T S O C E T N E P J L M H S E
W N S T E P H E N B X Z L J K
P O R T I C O H P P H I L I P
N O M R E S V B B E L I E V E
```

Find the answers on page 158

CROSSWORD PUZZLE

ACROSS

4. How many disciples were together in Jerusalem? (Acts 2:14)
5. Peter called Jesus the _____ when he spoke to the Jewish leaders (Acts 4:11)
7. The disciples received the Holy Spirit at _____ (Acts 2:1–4)
8. Who did Stephen see standing at the right hand of God? (Acts 7:55)
10. Gamaliel told the Jewish leaders that if the disciples' plan was from God, the leaders would be _____ against God (Acts 5:38–39)
11. Whose words from the Psalms did Peter quote in his sermon at Pentecost? (Acts 2:25)
12. Stephen was full of God's grace and _____ (Acts 6:8)

DOWN

1. When Peter and John healed the beggar, what was it time for? (Acts 3:1)
2. Where did the disciples often preach about Jesus? (Acts 5:42)
3. The first Christians ate meals together, shared with people in need, and met at the _____ every day (Acts 2:45–47)
6. When Peter and John were arrested for preaching, five _____ men believed in Jesus (Acts 4:4)
9. The disciples did so many miracles that people brought their sick friends to the streets hoping Peter's _____ would fall on them (Acts 5:15)

Find the answers on page 158

Quiz 19
A NEW FOLLOWER

One of the greatest followers of Jesus was a man who at first *hated* Christians. God had a very special plan for this man to take the good news to people in different parts of the world. We can read his story and his teachings through his writings in the New Testament.

THE QUESTIONS BELOW ARE ABOUT A VERY SPECIAL FOLLOWER OF JESUS AND THE FIRST MISSIONARIES.
How many questions can you answer?

1. **What did a proud Pharisee named Saul do to the early Christians? (Acts 8:3)**
    a) he stole their donkeys
    b) he burned their homes
    c) he made fun of them in the streets
    d) he threw them in prison

2. What did God tell Ananias to do? (Acts 9:10–15)

a) arrest Saul to keep him from attacking the Christians

b) baptize Saul in the Jordan River

c) heal Saul's blindness so he could become a great missionary

d) speak to Saul on the road to Damascus

3. What was Saul's name changed to? (Acts 13:9)

a) Paul

b) Peter

c) Simeon

d) Samuel

4. Who was the first to travel with Paul on his missionary journeys? (Acts 12:25)

a) Cornelius

b) Thomas

c) Barnabas

d) Lazarus

5. Which of these things did not happen to Paul during his missionary travels? (2 Corinthians 11:25)

a) he was beaten with rods

b) he was crucified

c) he was stoned

d) he was shipwrecked three times

6. **Paul said he counted everything as a loss compared to what? (Philippians 3:8)**
   a) being a Pharisee
   b) preaching the good news
   c) obeying the Ten Commandments
   d) knowing Jesus Christ

7. **After being rich and poor, powerful and weak, what did Paul learn? (Philippians 4:12–13)**
   a) "I am better because of it"
   b) "I am happier with less"
   c) "I can do all things through Christ who gives me strength"
   d) "I can rely on my own strength"

8. **Who did Paul say is the image of the invisible God? (Colossians 1:13–15)**
   a) the disciples
   b) Jesus, God's Son
   c) the church
   d) the angels

Find the answers on page 159

FILL IN THE BLANKS

Here is an important verse from the apostle Paul.
Try to fill in as many blanks as you can
without looking at your Bible!

But for that very reason,

_____ showed me mercy.

And I am the worst of _____.

He showed me mercy so that

_____ Jesus could show

that he is very patient.

I was an example for those who

would come to believe in _____.

Then they would

receive _____ life.

(1 Timothy 1:16 NIrV)

Find the answers on page 159

CROSSWORD PUZZLE

ACROSS

1. The non-Jews God wanted Paul to share the good news with (Acts 9:15)
3. Which of Paul's relatives saved him when the Jews were trying to kill him? (Acts 23:16)
5. Where did Paul and Barnabas speak in Iconium? (Acts 14:1)
6. Where did Jesus speak to Saul (Paul), blinding him with a bright light? (Acts 9:3)
9. Which church sent out the first missionaries? (Acts 13:1–3)
10. What did Paul say makes us right with God? (Romans 5:1)
11. Paul told us that we should always be full of _____ in the Lord (Philippians 4:4)
12. Paul and Barnabas taught and _____ the word of the Lord together (Acts 15:35)

DOWN

2. Where did Paul spend three years on his missionary journey? (Acts 20:17, 31)
4. Which tribe of Israel was Paul from? (Romans 11:1)
7. What king did Paul speak to when he was in prison? (Acts 26:1–3)
8. Paul's son in the faith (1 Timothy 1:2)

Find the answers on page 159

WORD SEARCH
Can you find all the words?
Words may be forward, backward, or up-and-down.

PAUL   SAUL   SILAS

ANTIOCH   BARNABAS   PREACH

GENTILES   DAMASCUS   TIMOTHY

MISSIONARY   ANANIAS   ETERNAL LIFE

```
P C H B P R E A C H K H M N N Q
H G Q E T E R N A L L I F E W A
B A R N A B A S T C H N K D T N
K V B M I S S I O N A R Y D F T
S N M L U A P T J W L U A S W I
I K D A M A S C U S F G R M S O
L F G A N A N I A S M H F N B C
A K B W T H P D V N H S A L T H
S T M Q D M Y H T O M I T D S K
G N T M N G E N T I L E S N V S
```

Find the answers on page 159

Quiz 20
JOHN TELLS US ABOUT HEAVEN

Many people were becoming Christians, and the religious leaders treated Jesus's followers badly. The disciple John was sent away to try to keep him from sharing the good news. But God's plans were bigger. God showed John what heaven is like, and he wrote down what he saw for us!

HOW MANY QUESTIONS CAN YOU ANSWER ABOUT JOHN, HEAVEN, AND THE BOOK OF REVELATION?
Use your Bible if you need to.

1. **Where did John write the book of Revelation? (Revelation 1:9)**
   a) the Valley of Lebanon
   b) the island of Patmos
   c) the Lake of Gennesaret
   d) the Tower of Babel

2. What did John say about Jesus? (Revelation 1:7)

a) "He is in Galilee"
b) "He is going to Jerusalem"
c) "He is staying in heaven forever"
d) "He is coming with the clouds"

3. What sound did John hear? (Revelation 1:10)

a) a loud voice that sounded like a trumpet
b) a loud boom that sounded like a drum
c) a loud noise that sounded like a train
d) a loud choir singing songs

4. What was John told to do? (Revelation 1:11)

a) take pictures of what he saw
b) pay close attention to what he saw
c) write down what he saw
d) close his eyes

5. How was John allowed to see into heaven? (Revelation 4:1)

a) through a crack in the floor
b) through a window
c) through a door
d) through a telescope

6. **What was around the throne that John saw in heaven? (Revelation 4:3)**
   a) a tree
   b) a rainbow
   c) a cloud
   d) a colorful window

7. **What does Revelation 22:5 say we will not need in heaven?**
   a) food and water
   b) toys and books
   c) light from a lamp or the sun
   d) pianos and organs

8. **What important message did Jesus tell John? (Revelation 22:20)**
   a) "I am your Lord"
   b) "I created you"
   c) "I am your Shepherd"
   d) "I am coming soon!"

Make as many words as you
can out of the letters in

REVELATION

_____   _____

_____   _____

_____   _____

_____   _____

_____   _____

_____   _____

_____   _____

_____   _____

WORD SEARCH
Can you find all the words?
Words may be forward, backward, up-and-down, or diagonal.

RAINBOW	SOON	THRONE
CLOUDS	TRUMPET	REVELATION
LIGHT	JOHN	HEAVEN
PATMOS	ISLAND	VOICE

```
      C J         I H
    A J L A C B O R D C K
  E A J Y A O D T Y E L P A J Y
  N I R O E V B U L A V E I R H S A
  M S U H S O O N D P E A W G U L K
C U L S N L I E D T S L R O I H N E
H E A V E N C W A N L A T B E G T
I T N O H K E N O R H T B N Z R A
N D S P A T M O S H I T I E N
  A W S G I L U M O M A A
    T R U M P E T N S R A
      C S A     H O L
```

Find the answers on page 160

ACROSS

2. John saw seven gold _____ (Revelation 1:12)
6. What flashed around the throne in heaven? (Revelation 4:5)
10. Who will see Jesus when He returns? (Revelation 1:7)
11. Jesus told John not to be what? (Revelation 1:17)
12. Jesus said He would make all things _____ (Revelation 21:5)

DOWN

1. God says He is the Alpha and _____ (Revelation 1:8)
3. What will we never have in heaven? (Revelation 22:5)
4. What flows from the throne of God in heaven? (Revelation 22:1)
5. Who was sent to show John the revelation? (Revelation 1:1)
7. What are the 12 gates in heaven made of? (Revelation 21:21)
8. God is _____ to receive glory and honor (Revelation 4:11)
9. How many churches was John told to send his book to? (Revelation 1:11)

Find the answers on page 160

ANSWER KEY

QUIZ 1: THE FIRST FAMILY

1. d   2. a   3. b   4. c   5. c   6. d   7. c   8. d

```
A V L O B A I F L E H U
D E S C E N D A N T S R
A G F N R G T M E I M E
N E O F E K N I T G N A
O T S R I F A L A E V E
L A G U T W T Y S N O G
J B N I U L E B A O I S
Y L R T A C R N D C F E
M E T H U S E L A H E T
L S H N I A C I M T L H
```

QUIZ 2: GOD STARTS OVER

1. a   2. b   3. c   4. b   5. c   6. d   7. a   8. c

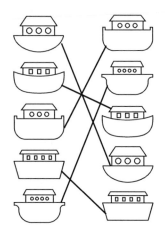

H D S M **N O A H** K L O S **H**
M E H S C G M S C D G R **A**
F L O O D H T G H K D E **M**
M B N B M E W D **J A P H E T H** Q W K B X Z
A R Q K M W B **P R O M I S E** K B R **D L O H**
R H D G R T **I S A A C** B N M S C **S A R A H**
K B D Q D L L P **A B R A H A M** T P L X N T
K H G N **N A M E** T K L P G H R T K F G R E

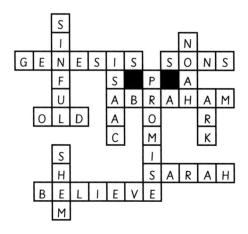

QUIZ 3: THE CHOSEN PEOPLE

1. d   2. b   3. d   4. a   5. d   6. b   7. c   8. c

```
Q R S T E W R P S D C B D T R S
R E B T R K L A D D E R S R E H
L L E W J A C V E S A U G I W E
P R O M I S E L A B W G S C Q E
K S N I W T P I S A A C M K M P
R E B E K A H N P S M A C O B Q
P R H L A B A N S E N J A C O B
```

```
      S T E W
      H     E           L
B E T H E L   L A B A N
      P       L         N
      H       A         D
    B L E S S I N G
      R       N
    P A D D A N       G
      E       E
      S       L     H
T W I N S   I S A A C
                    I
                    R
                    Y
```

QUIZ 4: JACOB GETS MARRIED

1. a   2. c   3. d   4. c   5. b   6. c   7. b   8. c

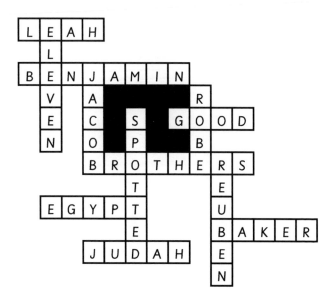

QUIZ 5: THE ISRAELITES GO TO EGYPT

1. c 2. c 3. b 4. c 5. c 6. d 7. b 8. c

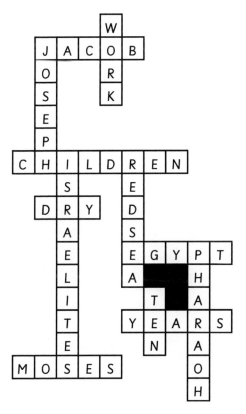

QUIZ 6:
MORE LEADERS FOR THE ISRAELITES

1. b 2. d 3. c 4. d 5. a 6. c 7. a 8. b

QUIZ 7:
MOTHERS, DAUGHTERS, AND SONS

1. b   2. c   3. d   4. a   5. c   6. a   7. b   8. d

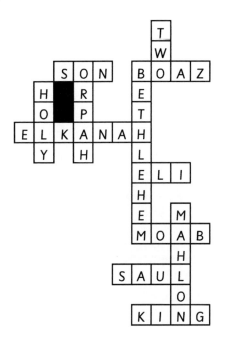

G O D   A N S W E R E D

H A N N A H ' S   P R A Y E R

```
G H K L H A N N A H R R D H T U R
R D S A M U E L G R N M D N D K T
A B F Q G R M E L K A N A H M P E
I M B O R P A H M N N A O M I W L
N S D Q F A M I N E W Z D O B Q I
B G R F I E L D B D Q G M O A B W
Q N R T T L Z A O B H N H B R D V
```

QUIZ 8: THE FIRST KINGS OF ISRAEL

1. b   2. a   3. b   4. c   5. d   6. c   7. d   8. a

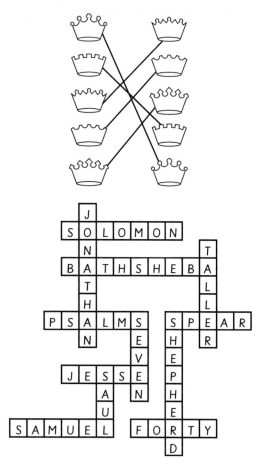

QUIZ 9:
TWO PROPHETS AND A QUEEN

1. b   2. d   3. c   4. c   5. a   6. d   7. b   8. b

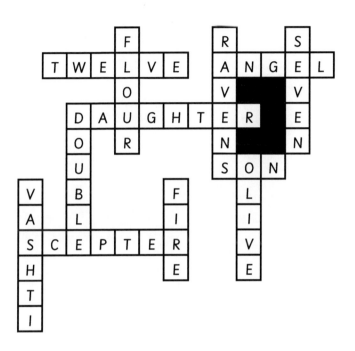

QUIZ 10: MORE PROPHETS

1. b   2. a   3. d   4. b   5. c   6. c   7. d   8. a

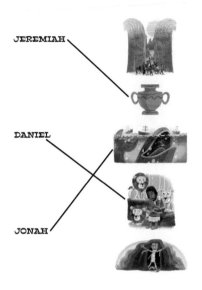

JEREMIAH

DANIEL

JONAH

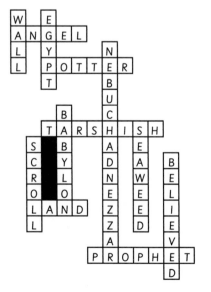

D N L **D A N I E L** M N **S**
J H D **W H S I F** K W Q **C**
E N L N **L I O N S** B D **R**
R H N B R F Y C S H G **O**
E W R **K R E T T O P** J **L**
M K B S D **P R A Y H O L**
I S M O U T H B F V N **L**
A **W E E P I N G** W N A **P**
H V **N I N E V E H** N H **V**
T R H S **T A R S H I S H**

QUIZ 11: A SAVIOR FOR THE PEOPLE

1. c 2. a 3. c 4. c 5. d 6. b 7. a 8. d

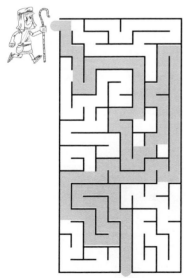

KD **SHEPHERDS** HMHB J
MHPPGKMPEEHSKRL O
ABRLT **GABRIEL** MQG H
RKNHSUS **JESUS** WQDN
YNBCDLRJT **ANNA** KLB
KNGLLEGNAVJLNPHR
SMS **SIMEON** KM **JOSEPH**
H **TEBAZILE** KZDZLWB
MSHS **MESSIAH** KLTND

QUIZ 12: THE TWELVE DISCIPLES

1. d   2. c   3. d   4. c   5. b   6. d   7. a   8. c

S I M O N   P E T E R

A N D R E W

J A M E S

J O H N

P H I L I P

B A R T H O L O M E W

M A T T H E W

T H O M A S

J A M E S
(son of Alphaeus)

S I M O N
(called the Zealot)

J U D A S
(son of James)

J U D A S   I S C A R I O T

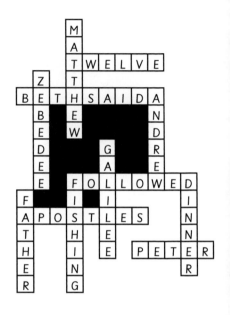

```
A P L R S H E L P E R S H P S G K N
N N T P I L I H P M T H F O L L O W
R G D K D I S C I P L E S K G Q H N
P L W R K L T J O H N J V R T V B L
H E C F E N F S E M A J K T N J P H
Q V T S T W J T T H O M A S J L D F
H Q G E K K N J M A T T H E W N T P
Q R T H R M B F I S H E R M E N J T
A P S Q G W A P O S T L E S M N R F
```

QUIZ 13:
JESUS PERFORMS MIRACLES
FOR THE PEOPLE

1. a 2. d 3. b 4. c 5. c 6. b 7. c 8. d

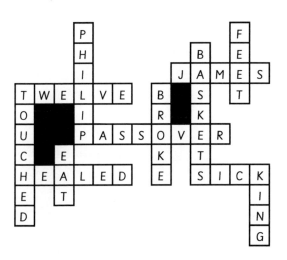

```
L B H E A L E R G H P T H F C T
O T R G H E V L E W T H T E J H
A K B P H I L I P N B C T E N O
V B S K D H S I F T S D W T B U
E S K B A S K E T S H D N B K S
S D T A N D R E W J T I M T H A
B J A I R U S K B Q D N V S T N
R E V O S S A P M N T H T L N D
D S W G H K J L B E L I E V E G
```

QUIZ 14: JESUS HEALS PEOPLE

1. b   2. c   3. a   4. d   5. d   6. a   7. c   8. b

Crossword answers: COAT, HEAVEN, FOLLOWED, SPIT, HAND, BEGGAR, RADAY(?), EVERYTY, DAVID, SEAK, BARTIMAEUS

Word search letters:

```
B D F G H F A E D K N S P E A K
N L P N B F S R A E Y F A I T H
B Z I R G H D M E R C Y T H N P
N E T N L P V N C R O W D T L V
K L G H D V F G B T O N G U E L
N B T G V C M O H C I R E J K T
B C R S A W B A R T I M A E U S
G B R T H R N B T H P H T D R N
S D R A H T A H P H P E M N T S
```

QUIZ 15: JESUS'S SPECIAL FRIENDS

1. c 2. b 3. a 4. d 5. c 6. b 7. c 8. d

QUIZ 16: JESUS AND NICODEMUS

1. d 2. b 3. c 4. d 5. c 6. d 7. a 8. c

"For __God__ so __loved__

the world that he __gave__

his one and only __Son__ ,

that whoever __believes__ in him

shall __not__ perish but have

__eternal__ __life__ ."

John 3:16 (NIV)

H M D G N I C O D E M U S N C M S L
Q R W R L T I G N I G H T Q K L N O
H G S H S I W E J N B T Y N S W T V
P W B E L I E V E M W N R O B H L E
B V N G A G A I N T H S A V E D K L
R S S R E D A E L M W Q S T O N S H
M D L P N S Q U E S T I O N S N G T
B V K L J E S U S N M W O R L D G F

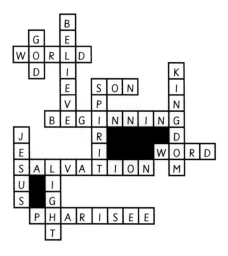

QUIZ 17: JESUS AND THE CROSS

1. a   2. c   3. b   4. b   5. d   6. d   7. a   8. c

_J_e_s_u_s_   _i_s_   _a_l_i_v_e!
✪ ❄ ▲ ◆ ▲   ❄ ▲   ❀ ● ❄ ❖ ❄

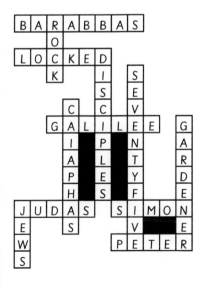

```
        H G K C O R
        K L B B T W
        D M A R Y G
        R C R L T R
    E T O M B Q U A K E T A L I P U
    X G N S I O R B H M B T W I L M
    M C I H S O W B W L G E R Y K A
    V P R I C A I A P H A S J N I T
    T E O B A I F S E T R U T W S M
    G O V E R N O R Q R D F S H U T
        W N M E N E
        Z A A G E N
        J C R S W E
        U U B W O R
        D G Z A E D
        A O M B R L
        S I M O N G
        Y E P O K N
        D A H K L O
        J U S W E J
        O H N B E C
```

QUIZ 18:
THE DISCIPLES TEACH
THE FIRST CHRISTIANS

1. a   2. b   3. a   4. c   5. d   6. d   7. c   8. b

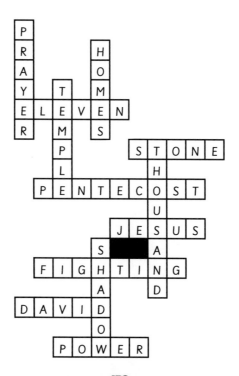

```
J K L M N B G R E T E P K L B
N O N K J Q H N N P R T Z B A
B C H W T N B L I A J Z K N P
B D N N K T R D H T N C R R T
S H G L M G A M A L I E L G I
B H L H O L Y S P I R I T R Z
T S O C E T N E P J L M H S E
W N S T E P H E N B X Z L J K
P O R T I C O H P P H I L I P
N O M R E S V B B E L I E V E
```

```
P
R         H
A         O
Y   T     M
E L E V E N
R   M     S
    P         S T O N E
    L         H
  P E N T E C O S T
              U
          J E S U S
        S ▓ A
    F I G H T I N G
        A     D
  D A V I D
        O
      P O W E R
```

QUIZ 19: A NEW FOLLOWER

1. d 2. c 3. a 4. c 5. b 6. d 7. c 8. b

But for that very reason,
___God___ showed me mercy.
And I am the worst of ___sinners___.
He showed me mercy so that
___Christ___ Jesus could show
that he is very patient.
I was an example for those who
would come to believe in ___him___.
Then they would
receive ___eternal___ life.

(1 Timothy 1:16 NIrV)

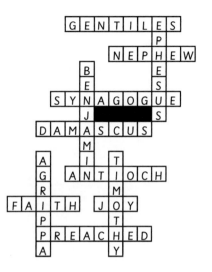

```
P C H B P R E A C H K H M N N Q
H G Q E T E R N A L L I F E W A
B A R N A B A S T C H N K D T N
K V B M I S S I O N A R Y D F T
S N M L U A P T J W L U A S W I
I K D A M A S C U S F G R M S O
L F G A N A N I A S M H F N B C
A K B W T H P D V N H S A L T H
S T M Q D M Y H T O M I T D S K
G N T M N G E N T I L E S N V S
```

QUIZ 20:
JOHN TELLS US ABOUT HEAVEN

1. b   2. d   3. a   4. c   5. c   6. b   7. c   8. d